IN REST

Sabbath Poems

JUSTIN McROBERTS

PUNCHLINE
PUBLISHERS

First paperback edition June 2024.

Cover Design / Illustration by Jon Diventi (jondiventi.com)
Book design by Asya Blue Design

ISBN 978-1-955051-39-2 Paperback
ISBN 978-1-955051-40-8 Ebook

Published in association with Punchline Publishers
www.punchlineagency.com

justinmcroberts.com
@justinmcroberts

Sabbath Keeping has shaken loose quite a bit in me, much of which I keep tucked away in my own chest; it's for me. So, neener. Like Mary, I am learning to treasure the offerings and counsels of angelic and Divine care. Appropriately, that's a posture I've learned in the practice of rest. The pieces that make up this short volume started coming alive after a long season of holding and cherishing what I'd received in rest rather than trying to pass them on. I worked to write them in the way I received them. Less like teachings and more like the soft knock of a friend you were already expecting at your door.

I found it fascinating that they grew up in poetic form. I suppose the delicacy and precision of their shape in my soul required a kind of care in communication poetry calls a writer to.

Poetry, like Sabbath Rest, asks both reader and writer to slow down and even stop; to pay attention to what is and appreciate the reality beneath the words I'm using. Particularly when that Reality is sacred in nature. Said otherwise, poetry is what happens when language runs up against A Reality it cannot grasp. Poetry is the shape words take after they have broken on the shores of The Thing I was chasing with my words (or That Which Language Seeks). Poetry is a way I describe things I want to set free from my descriptions (so, I can continue to believe there is more than I can name). Which makes Poetry so much like Love, itself; ever-present and perpetually allusive.

I share those thoughts because I've been hesitant to call these "poems." In fact, there was a point in the process of this project at which a editor said something like "these look like poems, but…" And I hit pause to take a moment and remember a few things my soul already knew. One of those things is that she was likely right, in a way.

They aren't great poems.
I'm not a great poet.
Not for the people
editors and publishers
might want
to give poetry to.

And that rhymes for me, historically.
(that's a really cheap poetry joke)

I've never been considered
"the best"
at anything I've done.

Ever.

Student - made B's and a few C's and the occasional A.
Youth Worker- So fun. Got fired.
Pastor - (this is a whole book but, in short) So fun. Got fired.
Musician - Always an opener, associated with those who headlined.
Author - Always an opener, associated with those who headlined.

Never "the best."
But I've never cared.

I've just done what I do
and believed it was enough
for the people it meets
and the One Who Holds It All Together.

And I think you might resonate with that sentiment:

"This is what
I have to give.
Is this enough?"

Appropriately,
that's the heart of Sabbath:
Believing who you are
and what you have
is enough.

(and maybe even lovable)

So, I wrote you some poems.
Because I want to help you
believe that who you are
and what you have
is enough

(and maybe even lovable)

For busbee. I miss you and the way you turned each phrase.

I have heard it said
"Evil never rests."
If that is so,
then I will become
like the thing
I have committed myself
to undoing.

I will counter evil,
not by out-dueling it
blow for blow
but by becoming unlike it;

I will learn
and practice
and teach
a better way;
A way that is
not controlling
but loving,
not anxious
but joyful,
not violent
but generative,
not hurried
but attentive,
not vengeful
but long-suffering.

Evil may not rest.
I will.

Because I do not stop
until I am worn out,
or something goes wrong
or something falls apart,
the only time
I take a long look at my life
is when I'm in the dark
or in distress.

This keeps me
from seeing clearly
the gift it is
to be alive.

In rest,
I gain room
for other people
as they actually are.

In rest, I see
that what I've been trained
to call "busyness"
has meant thinking
I have no time
for the oddities
and contradictions
of your story.

In rest,
I see the ways such "busyness"
has numbed me to
the pain and confusion
that often accompany
the complexity
of being human.

In rest,
I gain a lovingly critical vision
for the pace and pattern
of my life
and efforts.

In rest,
I see how the crush and hurry
that comes with being work-centered
requires that I become a driven thing,
bent towards finishing
and then moving on to what's next.

This comes
at the cost
of my humanity
and, as a consequence,
yours, as well.

Which is to say
in rest,
I remember
you and I
are not machines
and that we must
remind each other of that.

In rest,
I become aware of you
not as a puzzle piece
but as a Person;
confoundingly whole,
and beguiling.

In rest,
I can be attentive to you
not as a threat to my peace
or a distracting nuisance,
but as surprising
and worth stopping for.

In rest,
I become available to you
not as I need you to be
but as you are
and as you need to be.

In rest,
I become more
internally spacious;
more peacefully receptive.

In rest,
I cease
from giving my attentions
to the things
I am told
I should attend to
and, instead,
I pay attention
to What Is.

Rest is
the active denial
of entities and ideologies
that would seek to shape me
into a useful tool used to build
more entities and ideologies
that shape you into a tool.

Rest is
an act of resistance
against forces and powers
that would have me submit
my human wholeness
to inhuman schemes
which, in turn,
dehumanize you.

In rest,
I acknowledge that
it is not enough
to think of myself
as a victim
of my own aspirations
or my own desires.

In rest, I know that
I am the object
of an intentional,
coordinated,
well-funded
and cleverly disguised effort
to make me something
less than human.

In rest,
I learned to say "No,
I am more
than the uses
you have for me."

In rest,
I learn to differentiate
between longing
and anxiousness.

In rest
I remember the difference
between moving away from fear
and moving toward hope and joy.

In rest,
I recognize and confess
that urgency sets the agenda
for far too many of my days

In rest,
I can sense
the presence The Urgent
in the pace
of the world around me;
specifically
the world in which
my work takes place.

In rest,
I recognize and confess that,
so long as I am in motion
and busy with work,
I am susceptible to
the pressure and rhythm
of The Immediate.

In rest,
I free myself of Immediacy's
quick and anxious grasp
giving my heart space
and permission
to say "This is what I want.
This is what I need."

In rest,
I learn to parse
good from good.
When the windstorm
of external energies
and controlling agendas fades,
I can see that the dividing line
is my desire.

In rest, I hear You saying
"What do you want?
Where do you want to go.
I will go with you."

In rest,
I experience choice
as a formative practice
and learn the power
of my own will
to shape my days.

In rest,
I learn that
Desire and Decision
are the hammer and chisel
by which I chip away
everything that is not me.

In rest,
I learn the secret
that there are no secret meanings
and no latent purposes
waiting in each moment,
for me to discover and discern
once I've become
wise and worthy.

I remember that,
in-dwelt by the Spirit
of The One Who Holds All Things Together,
I am the bringer
of meaning and purpose
to each moment.

In rest,
I remember that
I am not the accumulation
of the preferences and interests
formed in me by the ads.

Instead,
as I make intentional
and thoughtful choices
(even and especially
between differing goods),
my character and interests are formed.

In rest,
I see that choice
does more than
reveal what I want;
the act of choice
shapes and reshapes
what I want.

In rest,
I learn that
it is by choosing differently
that I learn to want differently.

In rest,
even that which is
unfinished and incomplete
can be celebrated
as it is
and for the work
it has taken
to make it so.

In rest
I learn to differentiate
between who I wish I was
and who I am becoming.

Which is to say,
I learn to see the difference
between fearful projection
and embodied hope.

In rest
I learn to see
that my "ideal self"
is a ghost,
born from anxiousness and envy;
a ghost that,
left unnamed and unchecked,
might haunt me for years
from the dark and noisy spaces
between tasks and achievements.

In rest,
I come to see
that moving
from false self to true self
requires more than hard work
and more than expectant waiting;
it requires the transformation of my will
at the hands of a Loving God
and faithful friends.

In rest,
I see my becoming
(my growth and maturity)
take root in the knowledge
of my Belovedness;
I am loved as I am
and that sets me free
for the work and process
of growth and becoming.

In rest,
I practice the knowledge
that the person I wish I was
is only an idea
and that the simplicity
and flatness of that idea
are an affront to
the wildness of my Humanity.

Rest is a confession
and a communication
I make to those nearest me
that I am aware
of my limitations,
that I am comfortable with them
and that they can be, too.

Rest prepares me
to receive the love of those
who know I am finite;
those who know
that I can only do so much
and that they will
only "get so much of time."

Rest trains my heart
to receive and care
for those around me
who are finite;
I remember
that they can only do so much
and that I will only have them
for so long.

In rest,
I pause from my making
to acknowledge that
I, too, am being made;
by systems and wills
and forces and agendas
often without my awareness of them
and even without my consent.

In rest,
I create space
in which I consciously choose
which Powers have access to me,
and which should not.

In rest,
I experience
the power and freedom
of the word “no.”

“No, I won’t do that.”
“No, I won’t be able to make it.”
“No, I won’t get that done today.”

In time,
my “yes”
can become meaningful.

In rest,
my body has freedom
to ache.

Just as grief and sadness
need their space and time
lest they take it
from somewhere else,
so it is
with the pain
and weariness
in my body.

Rest is a choice I make
to enter into
the rhythms of nature
that flow from
and are rooted in
The Way Of Things.

Rest is both
a confession
that I am limited
in my energies/abilities
and a declaration
that the places I've chosen
to invest myself
are worth sacrificing
other efforts and opportunities for.

In rest
I remember that
it is not work
that is poisonous;
it is fear and ego
that poison all good gifts.

In rest,
I remember that
work is not
an enemy of my soul.
I remember that
work is a gift
and learn to desire it as such.

In rest,
I allow, invite
and even command
my conscious mind
to bend an ear
and pay attention
to the whisperings,
longings,
complaints
and rhythms
of my subconscious,
my body
and the living world around me.

In doing so,
I become less mechanical,
less tame
and more fully human.

In rest,
I have time
to attend to my soreness,
injury and imbalance
so that,
more than simply fixing
or avoiding
pain and discomfort,
I can learn
what there is to be learned
from it.

In rest,
I learn to take joy
in the best of my efforts,
not because they were deemed
worthy or “enough“
by those I offer them to
but because I see
the best of myself in them
and like who I am becoming.

In rest,
I put even the most,
urgent and important works of my life
in their place;
as aspects of
and expressions of
my healthy wholeness.

In rest,
I learn to “hear” and “feel” my body
so that I can listen and care
in ways that I cannot
when in a posture
of perpetual use.

In rest,
I practice the realty that
while the "world spins on,"
I do not need to.

I remember that,
regardless of the gravity and delicacy
of a particular a moment
(or even an entire season),
My life must not
be defined by urgency.

In rest,
I practice the reality that,
while I cannot will
the chaos of the world around me to be still,
I can instruct my own soul.

In rest,
I hope to find an anchor in my soul
so that, when others are
tossed and overwhelmed
by the gravity and urgency
of a moment
or a season,
they can find a place
of stillness and peace with me.

Rest is
the conscious choice
to peak into
or step into
or even immerse myself
in a Story grander, richer
and more beautiful
than a story of my own devising;
a story about my usefulness.

In rest,
I can kindly greet
my False Self,
my adaptive strategies,
and my defense mechanisms.
I can find thankfulness in me
for the ways I've
(often quite appropriately)
navigated and responded
to the turbulence of things.

In rest
I find the freedom
to feel what I'm feeling
and, as I do so,
learn what I actually think
about what I feel.

In rest,
the different facets of my soul
have space and freedom
to differentiate themselves
from one another
so that, as they work in relationship
rather than competition and confusion,
I can live more wholly.

In rest,
I cease from building
and defending myself.
I let my guard down.
In the quiet near my center,
I find a longing
to trust my Self to better,
more capable hands.

In rest,
worry and anxiousness
have time to settle
like dust and silt,
and I can hear,
in my depths,
whispered assurances
of a beautiful tomorrow.

In rest
I can enjoy slowness
without resenting
the faster pace
of other days.

In rest,
I can sit in stillness
without thumbing my nose
at movement
and productivity.

In rest,
I learn to live
less divided
and with less tension
between the varying aspects
of my Wholeness.

In rest,
I can regain the joy
with which
I originally
took up
my obligations
and burdens;

In rest,
I reclaim
the joy stolen
by worry
and haste.

In rest,
my fears can be met,
not with a noise
loud enough
to drown them out,
but with a silence
deep enough
to expose
how small
they are.

In rest,
I grow comfortable
with only having
partial truths to tell.

In rest,
my soul learns to discern
anxiousness from urgency
and urgency from calling.
I remember that,
while I am grieved
and sometimes compelled
by the conditions
of the world
I choose to care for,
it is not "my" world
to care for.

In rest,
I remember that my work
is a way I participate
in a larger redemptive work
that will claim me as well.

In rest,
I uproot my motives
and my actions
from the soil
of mathematical analysis
to let whatever fruit has grown
on that vine
wither and be pruned.

In rest,
my soul learns to love.

In rest,
the gifts I've been given
(in love, by God)
can simply be gifts
rather than training
or equipment
with which I must
do something
for someone else.

In rest,
it is enough
to receive good things
from God.

In rest,
it is enough
to receive God.

In rest,
I can hear
the voice in me
that demands "results"
and "achievement"
and "success"
without hearing
an enemy.

Silence and stillness
acquaint me with that voice.
and I begin to hear
the fear in it.
I begin to feel
empathy for myself.

Rather than the voice
of an angry boss
or a disappointed parent,
in the quiet of rest,
I hear these demands
coming from
the part of my soul,
that wonders and worries
if I can be Truly Loved
when I do not produce.

In rest,
I practice a posture
of receptivity
and openness

I find myself
humble,
vulnerable,
unafraid
(or, at least,
less afraid)

In rest,
I can receive
the good gifts
I might otherwise miss
while I find myself
too proud,
too protected,
too scared.

Rest,
like work,
is an expression
of power;

The power
to say “no”
to what is
obligatory and productive
The power
to say “yes”
to that
which gives life
and is joyous.

In rest,
I can confess
without shame
that I am not
everything I wish I was,
that I've not always
applied myself fully,
and that even
my best efforts
fall short of ideals
I've aimed for.

Rest is
an expression
and declaration
of hope.
That when my efforts cease,
all things are held together
by Loving Hands
more capable than mine
and that I am part
of "All Things."

In rest,
I learn that
love is not handed over
like a medal
at the end of a race I've won
(or a game I've played well).

In rest,
I practice believing
I am loved
because I exist.

In rest,
I scandalously disengage
from the defining battles
of the moment I'm in.

In rest,
I declare that
as vital
and important
and urgent
and large
as any of these
movements
or issues
or crises are,
none of them own me.

In rest,
I emphasize
my own well-being

Every other day,
I will be helpful,
and useful
and present
to the work
of making the world around me
a more beautiful,
more just,
and more peaceful place.

On this day,
I simply want
to attend to the world within me;
that I might find,
in my own soul,
more beauty,
more justice
and more peace.

In rest,
I not only make room
for joys I already know live in me,
I give my soul space
to reveal joys
I did not know
I had (or desired).

In rest,
my capacity for joy
and the appreciation I feel
for my own life
expand to include
new pleasures,
new hopes
and new dreams.

In rest,
I am invited to step away
from networks of connections
and the social mathematics
of transaction.

In rest,
I practice believing
I am valuable
because I am Beloved
and that no offering of mine
(or inadequacy)
can change that.

In rest,
I make room
for soul-work
I don't recognize
I have a need for.

In rest,
I let my soul, mind, and body
tell me what they need.

In rest,
I gain the loving perspective
to consider the seeds
I have been planting
in my own soul.

In rest,
I can evaluate
the health of
what is growing in me
and then either
joyfully and wisely
plant more of the same
or patiently correct myself
and begin planting
something better.

In rest,
I can confess
I am
(and have been)
hurt.

In rest,
I confess also
that I am okay
and will be.

Rest is a confession
that some things
have been too much for me;
that I have been
overpowered
and overwhelmed.

In rest,
I give myself permission
to be inconclusive
and unresolved.

In rest,
I give myself permission
to not have answers,
to not know,
to not see,
to not understand
and to not control.

In rest,
I cease from holding it together
and let myself to be held;
held in Divine Hands
which hold all things in place.

In rest,
the cold mathematics
of business and productivity
give way to a sacred accounting;
Something less like
crunching data
and more like
the soft pressure
of taking my own pulse.

In rest,
I weigh my options
on a scale of joy
and weigh my choices
on a scale of happiness.

In rest,
I count hours and dollars,
not by their raw number,
but by the weight of each
on my soul
and my psyche.

In rest,
the mathematics of life
hinge not on "How much?" or "How many?"
but on deeper and better questions;
questions like
"Am I alive?"

In rest,
I exhale and find
there is more room in me
than I knew.
There is more strength in me
than I knew.
There is more peace in me
than I knew.

In rest,
I exhale and find
there is simply more of me
than I knew.

In rest,
I exhale and find
I have grown.

Rest is a confession
to those who love me
that I am aware
of my own limitations,
and that I am
comfortable with them.

Rest is a challenge
to those who might use me
that I am aware
of my own limitations,
and that I am
comfortable with them.

In rest,
my heart can
more clearly discern
legitimate crises
from mere annoyance.

In rest,
I ease into a knowledge
of the things
I naturally
and passionately
care about.

In rest,
the chaotic
and anxious
and angry Voice
that tells me
I must care about "this"
or I must care about "that"
is swallowed up
like a leaf in a stream.

In rest,
I remember that
there is too much to care about
for one day
or one week
or even a lifetime.

In rest,
I remember that
when I am overextended,
I diminish myself
and my capacity to care
wisely and well.

In rest,
I learn and remember that
discerning which things
I can give myself to
is a question of limitation;
I only live so long
and only have so much to offer
while I'm here.

I came to rest
because I was exhausted.
I long to make rest
a matter of choice.

I long for rest
to be the place
from which I start;
the root of fruitful work
and healthy relationships.

I've read that
God "rested
from all the work
he had done."

I never feel done.
That makes rest a choice.

So much of what I do
feels (and often is)
very important;
as if every task
and every project
is a dragon I must slay.

Putting important things down
can be so hard.

Which is to say,

Choosing rest means
staring "the dragon" in the eyes,
putting down my sword,
turning my back on it.
and saying,
"You are not
more important
than my health.
And when I am rested,
connected and clear-headed,
you don't stand a chance."

In rest,
I can take account
of the things
I have stolen from myself
in haste and in shame.

In rest,
I can grieve that loss
and then,
having let myself
hurt a little while,
ready myself to receive
good gifts
as (and when)
they are offered.

In rest,
I can gather the hours
that have passed
and not only find
but enjoy
the rich beauty
that has been available to me
all along.

Rest is not
the absence of work.
Nor is rest a reward
for having achieved
and performed
and produced.
Rest is an
intentional and regular divorce
from those systems
that would seek to make
health and wholeness into rewards
rather than birthrights.

Rest is
a focused attention
to the pulse and heartbeat
of The Divine.

Rest is
the active remembrance
of my humanity.

Rest is
where and how
I acquaint and attach myself
to that which
gives my work meaning.

In rest,
I learn to distinguish
between core needs
and pesky wants.

Desire is good,
it simply isn't the same
as need.
They can feel the same
until I have the time
to more deeply listen
and attend
and weigh.

In rest,
the things I fear
catch up with me
along with the goodness
and sweetness
of my days.
When they do,
I can see
they are often smaller
and far fewer.
than my hurried
and harassed imagination
had made them.

I can also see that
some of these fears
are just trying to keep me alive;
calling my focused attention
towards things that might
truly steal life from me.

In rest,
my fears can find context
in the good and labyrinthine life
they are an integral part of.

In rest,
I have the time and space
to see my unfinished life
without shame.
in the absence
of the rush and buzz
that often marks my workdays,
I can take a sober look
at the landscape of my goings on
and call these things "good,"
even while being incomplete.

To rest
while in the midst of
a great work
communicates to others
as well as to my own soul,
a consciousness that I am
not the engine of the great work;
I am a participant
and a celebrant
and then a worker
and co-laborer.

To think of myself
as essential or necessary
is to idolize my own power.
The practice of Rest
helps to rescue me
from that idolatry;
freeing me
to humbly and thankfully
find my place
in the great work.

Rest is the active anticipation
of goodness;
a pause that says
"I know that I do not
have to know
what comes next
to believe and trust
there is good in it."

Rest is a declaration
that it is not my seeking
or working
or drilling down
that always exposes
or brings about goodness.
It is also my willingness
to stop and wait
and pay attention to what is, as it is,
that allows me to see goodness.

Rest is the oddly defiant hope
that there is Good Will
at the core of all things
and that, should I wait
instead of only work,
I will be caught up, held,
and sustained
by that Good Will.

In rest,
I recover my body.
Not just by attending
to my physical well-being,
but in receiving the permission
to be a physical being at all.

In rest,
I can choose
to see my body's health
in the same way I see
my mental and emotional health;
not as a matter of
putting myself back together
so I can get back to work,
and not as a useful tool
needing repair
in order to be useful again,
but as a blessed gift
to be cherished and enjoyed.

In rest,
I can remove pleasure
from its sad place
on the pile of discarded human experiences
labeled “sin: do not touch.”

All too often,
a body wracked by busyness
and numbed by stress
is met by a religious teaching
that would further deny
bodily joy and pleasure;
piling shame on top of exhaustion
and prescribing
(if not demanding)
disembodiment
as the “righteous path.”

In rest,
I pull a head of grain
off its stalk and eat it
because it’s what my body wants.
And when moralism
or religiosity flips its lid,
I can respond
“The Sabbath was made for man,
not man for the Sabbath.”

In rest,
I employ what Henry Nouwen called
"the ministry of disappointment;"
by saying "not today"
to most relationships.

In rest,
I close the door,
not only to
the demands and agendas
of jobs and agencies,
but even to people
I care about.

In rest,
I recognize that
the work of community
is still a work.
And like the other works in my life,
I am responsible to myself in it
as well as the work itself.

In rest,
I practice enjoying the promise
of a world made whole;
being fed by that hope
and acquiring a taste for it.

In rest,
I see that many of
the cultures I work in / around
have acquired an unhealthy taste
for human drama, itself;
the thrill of the fall and the chase.

Rest saves me
from the temptation
to enjoy the fight
simply because of the way I feel
while fighting.
Rest helps rescue me
from gleefully counting conflict
as victory.

In rest,
I come to more deeply believe
that shalom is possible
and is preferable to victory alone;
more soul satisfying
than the thrill of any battle
it might take to achieve it.

In rest,
I become acquainted
with my tiredness and its sources.
What would otherwise be
the dull ache
of nameless exhaustion,
masked by caffeine or gumption,
can be exposed and named.

In rest,
I can trace the lines
from my wits end
to the works,
relationships
and pattens
that have worn me out.

Then,
in rest,
I can gain altitude
over my own decisions,
learning to discern
and imagine
how I might live
with less tension,
less strife
and with more peace.

In rest,
my soul has permission
to prefer simplicity
over complexity;
To guiltlessly
pare down the things
I'm willing to hold,
even to one at a time.

In rest,
I don't need to critique
my broader culture
and it's penchant for confusion
or it's love of complication;
I can simply say
"Not me.
Not today."

In rest,
I catch up with myself
and become awake;
I feel and see
and smell and hear and taste
the life I'm in.
And when I do,
I find that it is charmed.

In rest,
I learn to see
the people I work with
as whole persons.
It is not the Work we share
or our drive for Productivity
that minimizes and dehumanizes;
often, it is my hurry.

In haste, I pass by and ignore.
In haste, I use and discard.
In haste, I make tools out of others' gifts
and the people who possess them.

Only a slower pace,
a longer pause
and a recognition
of my own humanity
cures me of my propensity
to reduce another person
to their utility.

In rest,
I remember and redeem
(in my own mind,
vision and experience),
the humanity
of the fully human people
my work places me near.

In rest,
I hear the words
I have been using
and realize they mean
far more
than the ways
I've been using them.

In rest,
tomorrow can wait
and none of its claims
on who I am supposed to be
have power over me.

In rest,
I command the urgencies
that would otherwise control me
"You will have your turn
when I tell you it's your turn.
Right now is not that moment."

In rest,
I remember and learn
that "Time" is the word I use
to explain the gift
of being here for a while.

In rest,
I get to reexamine
the way I experience
the passage and gift of Time, itself.
I remember and relearn
that time is not
a slave to urgency
or strategy.

In rest,
I learn to see that,
when I am cornered or driven
by urgency and strategy,
I am out of joint with Time.
Which is to say,
when I am cornered or driven
by urgency and strategy,
I am out of joint
with the gift it is
to be alive.

In rest,
work becomes meaningful
because it no longer "everything."
Meaning is contextually dependent.
When a "thing" becomes Everything,
meaning is lost.
Rest frames the work of my life
in the context of my Wholeness.

In rest,
I receive my tiredness
and even my exhaustion
in kindness;
as reminders of the places
my energies
and my efforts
had been welcomed.

In rest,
my anger has space
to be heard.
In rest,
anger helps me learn
the difference
between what is mine
to wrestle with
and what I can let go of.

In rest,
I tell my soul
“I am okay.
I am more than okay.”

In rest,
I am pressing my will
against the ways
I am told
I am not okay
by voices inside me
and many, many voices
outside of me.

In rest,
I can cease
from worry
that all my choices
were the right ones,

All things are held together
by Divine Hands
more loving and skilled than mine.
I am one of the things
being held together
by those hands.

ABOUT THE AUTHOR

Justin McRoberts is a writer, coach, speaker and retreat leader living in Martinez, CA. Justin is the author of 6 other books, including *Sacred Strides, It Is What You Make of It* and *Prayer: 40 Days of Practice.*

Printed in Dunstable, United Kingdom

67713671R00068